CUSTOM KETO DIET

ANURADHA SRIVASTAVA

ISBN 979-888546433-8

<u>Custom Keto Diet</u>

<u>Custom Keto Diet</u> Reviews - A Detailed Report On The Keto Weight Loss Program! Reviewed By Consumers Companion

Custom Keto Diet program - Everything about the keto weight loss program Custom Keto Diet discussed. Custom Keto Diet reviews with author details, meal plan, benefits, pros and cons.

Custom Keto Diet is a meal program that helps you practice your ketogenic lifestyle free from any confusion. The program is created by Rachel Roberts and it provides you with diet plans and lifestyle intervention that helps you to stick to the diet. It has caught the attention of thousands of people throughout the US and has earned a credible space in the market. This Custom Keto Diet review article will take you through how the book is different from several other programs

Custom Keto Diet Reviews- A Customized Keto Meal Program!

The Keto Diet is one diet that has become popular in recent times. It depends on the principle of ketosis, i.e. using the body's fat reserves, in order to create energy that we can use for our day to day activities. The diet achieves this by totally cutting out any carbohydrate consumption, so the body is forced to turn to its fat reserves for fuel.

Well, the Keto Diet sounds nice and fancy, but it may be a little difficult to implement for first-timers. What carbs do you cut out, and how? You can't just eliminate whole foods from your diet, that's asking for trouble. Fortunately, the Custom Keto Diet is here to help you. But is this useful or just another fad diet? Read this Custom Keto Diet review to find out.

Enter Caption

Product Name

Custom Keto Diet

Category

Weight Loss

Creator

Rachel Roberts

Main Benefits

With help the Ketosis, the process helps you to reduce fat

Duration

8-week

Price

$37.00

Availability

Only through the official website

<u>Official Website</u>

What is <u>Custom Keto Diet</u> program?

Today, weight loss methods are so many, that you're spoilt for choice when it comes to choosing a program and sticking to it. Problem is, not all the programs or diets are practical. Some call for pretty drastic measures, and you may not be ready for such measures at this point in your life.

Custom Keto Diet is your one-stop-place for a customized keto meal program that can help you achieve optimum levels of health. People usually try adopting a keto diet after reading about it online, but it isn't that easy.

You need to know what kind of foods you can or cannot include in your diet. You just can't discard foods because you see fit. Moreover, the problem with most diet plans on the internet is that they adopt a one-size-fits-all approach, instead of a tailored individual approach towards beating obesity and giving people individual meal plans.

The Keto Diet is one diet that has become popular in recent times. It depends on the principle of ketosis, i.e. using the body's fat reserves, to create energy that we can use for our day-to-day activities. The diet achieves this by totally cutting out any carbohydrate consumption, so the body is forced to turn to its fat reserves for fuel.

Though it might sound fancy it can be a little chaotic for a first-timer. You might be confused about your meal plans, workout routines, and much more. This is where Custom Keto Diet plans work miraculously. It aids to chart down a whole meal plan and other activities that will support your diet.

About the author

Custom Keto Diet was created by Rachel Roberts who had an extraordinary experience that led her to a ketogenic diet. It was along with her holistic team that included chefs, nutritionists, dieticians, and fitness consultants that she formed this plan. It took about 8 weeks for the program to be formed.

Her reflection on how every individual requires a customized diet for their body is the reason she decided to create the Custom Keto Diet Plan. most often people follow diets without having much knowledge of what best fits them. From her research and experience, she learned that a ketogenic diet can be customized and tailor-made for individuals and hence came up with the plan.

How does the Custom Keto Diet Plan work?

The way the Custom Keto Diet works is pretty simple. It is totally different from the one-size-fits-all diet plans that are readily available all over the internet. This diet plan works in a tailored manner, by taking into account your age, height, weight, and the kinds of foods that you eat, and how old you are.

The diet works in the following way.

First Step - You will have to fill in a few pieces of data about yourself. These include your age, gender, food preferences, workout intensity, weight, height, and desired weight. This helps the website understand your present status to analyze required calories, activity level, BMI, nutrition intake. This is the initial step to help prepare your exclusive Custom Keto Diet plan.

Second Step - After filling in the data and going through the analytics, you will be asked to enter your name and mail id after which you will be taken to the payment portal. Once you have purchased the plan, you will receive a mail with your custom keto diet plan.

Third Step - The final step is to keep up consistency in following the plan. You mustn't break in between. Be it the meal plans, or workout routines stick to the planner so that you can lose weight healthily. The plan provides a list of recipes, the grocery list, and the portion size of each meal.

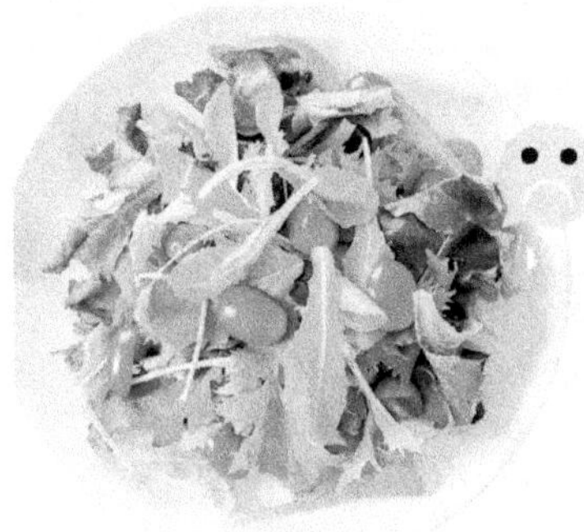

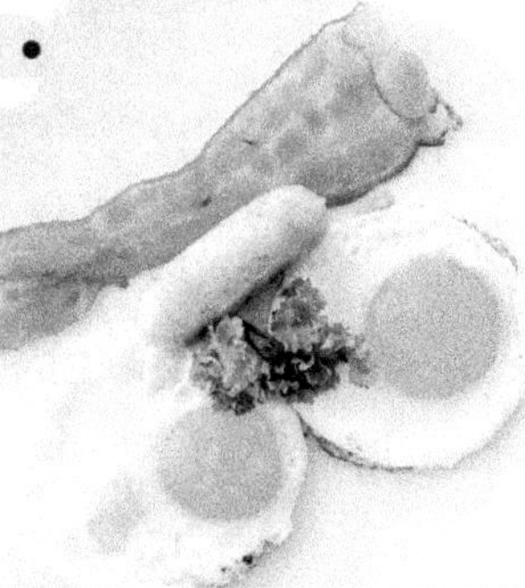

Enter Caption

What is the Custom Keto Diet Program?

- How does Custom Keto Diet work?

- Who is it for? Custom Keto Diet

- What can you get from Custom Keto Diet?

- Advantages of Custom Keto Diet

- Side Effects of Custom Keto Diet

- How much does the Custom Keto Diet Program cost?

- Custom Keto Diet Program Reviews: Conclusion

Custom Keto Diet Reviews

[Click Here to Order Custom Keto Diet Plan from the Official Website](#)

What is the Custom Keto Diet Program?

The Keto diet is currently a popular trend that most people are doing. However, there are a lot of risks to a person's health when the diet is not tailored for you

This is why the **Custom Keto Diet Program** is engineered to help millions of people who are trying to lose weight naturally and effectively.

Custom Keto Diet helps you understand the different types of food to eat to really help you lose weight and eliminate the fat in the stubborn areas of your body.

The Custom Keto Diet runs in an 8-week long program that tailors a customized meal plan for your specific body shape and type.

Custom Keto Diet also considers your lifestyle, how often you work out, how stressed you are, and unlike other keto diets, it considers your taste buds and your food preferences to ensure that you are enjoying each meal you are eating.

Dieting is not an easy thing to do, and it can be ineffective and unhealthy for the body.

This is why people who want to lose weight should be careful about what to follow, especially when this is just random information you see on the internet.

Diets should be based on your body type and lifestyle. Sometimes, it isn't enjoyable, especially when you restrict yourself from delicious foods.

But the creator of Custom Keto Diet, **Rachel Roberts,** wants individuals to really enjoy their diet and achieve successful results.

Custom Keto Diet can be very helpful because it allows you to fully commit to the meal plans because these are actually engineered based on your food preferences.

You don't have to say goodbye to the foods that you love while following this Custom Keto Diet program.

How does Custom Keto Diet work?

In recent studies published, it is found out that people who are into a <u>very low carbohydrate ketogenic diet (VLCKD)</u> are more prone to achieve a bigger percentage of weight loss chances rather than those assigned to a **low-fat diet (LFD).**

Therefore, the Custom Keto Diet program mainly revolves around the VLCKD concept. Custom Keto Diet Program helps in significantly increasing the fat burning process in the body.

Custom Keto Diet decreases your appetite and prevents you from craving more even when you have eaten enough for your body.

Custom Keto Diet is easy to prepare, and you don't have to be a professional cook to be able to prepare the meals.

Custom Keto Diet Program works without having the need to do intense workouts or exercises.

To know how the keto diet works, there are 4 mistakes you need to stop making to ensure a successful weight loss.

First, you need to stop not being in a calorie deficit. This means you should enjoy taking in calories because the body actually needs them to stimulate fat loss.

The second mistake would be having a severe calorie restriction that gives you slower metabolism.

So, when you stop your diet, the body then stores as much food as possible to prevent starvation.

Therefore, you get fatter after the diet. The third mistake is thinking calories are created equal.

This is why Custom Keto Diet teaches you more information that you can use in your diets and meal plans.

Lastly, having an unrealistic and overly restrictive diet will just burn you and your body out and lead to an unhealthy way of slimming down or becoming ineffective once you start getting out of the diet because no one can really live with that overly restrictive diet, can they?

Who is it for? Custom Keto Diet

Adult men and women who want to lose weight and eliminate the fats stored in their bodies are very much welcome to try the Custom Keto Diet program.

Rachel Roberts, the creator of **Custom Keto Diet**, has specifically engineered and customized this diet plan for you.

Individuals who want to lose weight in a natural and safe way should follow the Custom Keto Diet program.

Pregnant and nursing women are not allowed to follow the Custom Keto Diet program because it needs them to restrict their diet, which can be unhealthy for the baby or for the pregnant woman.

For people suffering medical conditions and are asked to eat healthy, please consult your doctor first before following the Custom Keto Diet program to ensure your safety.

What can you get from Custom Keto Diet?

When you avail the Custom Keto Diet program, you can get the whole package instantly.

Custom Keto Diet Program is packed with a complete set of materials that offer a wide coverage of information you can learn about a plus. It has detailed instructions to guide you through the **Custom Keto Diet** program and help you fully understand without getting confused with meals, recipes and can even help you make grocery shopping fun and easy.

Here is a list of materials you can get inclusive with the Custom Keto Diet program:

• The 8-week meal plan is used by nutritionists, personal trainers, and chefs to guarantee optimal progress in your weight loss journey. You do not have anything to worry about because the meals are actually easy to prepare.

The meals depend on your food preference, your lifestyle and are specially designed for your body type and shape. It is optimized for your own ideal calorie and macro intake.

• Instructions on how to customize your meals. This means you get to have a guided list of knowing what to eat, also customizing your meals depending on your food preference.

The meal plans offered in this Custom Keto Diet program have a lot of food variety, so there really are no problems in selecting the recipes you want to do.

• A grocery list that can help you save time in the supermarket. You can download this list for each week, and it already contains the ingredients you will need for the whole week of meals. It is that convenient.

• Fast Food Restaurant Guide fully equips you with knowledge about the right food to order when you are eating out.

This prevents you from getting tempted and having a cheat day during the 8-week program. Also, this information can help you in the long run, even after the Custom Keto Diet program.

• Keto Diet 101 is a manual of how the whole Custom Keto Diet program works. It contains everything you need to know about the whole process so you can grasp a full understanding of the program you are doing.

Different kinds of recipes are there in the Custom Keto Diet. Some of these recipes are for keto bacon, keto chocolate treats, keto savory foods, keto snacks, keto cookies, keto avocado foods, and many more to mention.

The **Custom Keto Diet** Program indeed offers a wide array of recipes that lets you eat delicious food while you are on a diet.

<u>Click Here to Order Custom Keto Diet Plan from the Official Website</u>

Advantages of Custom Keto Diet

When doing the Custom Keto Diet program, you are able to enjoy numerous benefits that will definitely boost your self-confidence.

Imagine wearing your clothes and feeling the fit become loose when you wear them. This one of the sure feelings you will get when you do the Custom Keto Diet program.

To enumerate, these are the amazing benefits that Custom Keto Diet can provide:

- A quick custom diet keto plan that can help you lose weight quickly and effectively. It can be used when preparing for an event or occasion because of how easy and quick the results show.

- Custom Keto Diet Program uses scientifically proven methods in choosing the right healthy food sources you can eat in your meal plans.

- Custom Keto Diet Program gives a detailed and well-instructed step-by-step guide on how to lose weight.

- Custom Keto Diet saves your time spent in supermarkets because of its helpful grocery list for each week's meal plans.

- Custom Keto Diet Plan is customized entirely on your food preference, body type, and lifestyle. So, it is more effective in losing weight, plus it helps you stay motivated in following the meal plan because the food you will eat is actually delicious.

- You are able to enjoy a more confident self as your body transforms into a healthier and prettier version of yourself.

- You are able to learn different kinds of recipes from appetizers, meals, and even desserts for your diet. This can help you eat anything you want without even feeling like you are on a diet because these recipes are keto-friendly.

- Custom Keto Diet Plan helps you choose the right food to order when you are in a restaurant so that you won't get tempted and have a cheat day while you are having a date or eating out with friends and family.

It is a very helpful guide that is useful even when the Custom Keto Diet program is over.

Like any other weight loss diets or products out there, it will be ineffective if the individual following does not fully commit to the **Custom Keto Diet** program.

Custom Keto Diet Program is important to stay disciplined and really commit to the weight loss Custom Keto Diet program to enjoy the optimal benefits it can provide.

<u>Click Here to Order Custom Keto Diet Plan from the Official Website</u>

Side Effects of Custom Keto Diet Plan:

Even when the Custom Keto Diet Plan is safe, there are still unavoidable side effects experienced by the people following the diet.

Regardless if it is specifically this **Custom Keto Diet** or other diets available for free, there really are side effects that come with it.

Side effects can be dizziness, feeling light-headed, low in energy, sleepy, and a weak feeling.

These side effects usually are felt when you first start doing the diet because your body is not used to the food intake you are doing.

After taking some time to adjust, your body switches back to its normal activity, and you will no longer feel the side effects.

How much does the Custom Keto Diet Program cost?

With everything you can get from the Custom Keto Diet program, it is surprisingly affordable.

You can get the whole Custom Keto Diet program package for only $37.

When compared to other keto diets available on the internet, the Custom Keto Diet Plan program stands out because the diet and meal plans it offers are customized to your body type, lifestyle, and, more importantly, food preferences.

This means you are able to eat delicious meals while still having a diet.

Custom Keto Diet is an amazing program that has helped thousands of men and women achieve their dream weight.

The **Custom Keto Plan** Diet Program has helped transform countless bodies into healthier, sexier, and better versions of themselves, all following a fast, effective and safe process.

Custom Keto Diet Plan helps you boost your self-confidence as you see yourself in the mirror now in your dream body weight.

Imagine wearing a fitting in your jeans and realizing they are looser in fit now.

The Custom Keto Diet Program is only available online, and you can download the materials included in the Custom Keto Diet program.

There are no physical copies sold for the Custom Keto Diet program, and everything will only be available for download.

The Custom Keto Diet Program fully guarantees a 100% satisfaction rate of the methods and recipes it uses.

People who have used Custom Keto Diet have applauded the program with positive reviews.

[Click Here to Order Custom Keto Diet Plan from the Official Website](#)

Custom Keto Diet Plan Reviews: Conclusion

Would you like to learn more about what kinds of food to lose weight and be healthier without having to say goodbye to your favorite food or deprive yourself of eating?

The Custom Keto Diet is engineered to give you a complete health transformation that will change your life for the better.

The Custom Keto Diet Plan will let you enjoy your whole weight loss process because you still get to eat delicious foods while having a diet.

This Custom Keto Diet program is perfect for people who want to lose weight quickly for events or occasions, too, as it offers quick results.

Custom Keto Diet is better to invest in a good and reliable diet program rather than following those free ones you see on the internet.

This ensures that your efforts do not go to waste, and investing in the **Custom Keto Diet Plan** has a big advantage since it customizes the whole 8-week program for your body type, food preference, and lifestyle.

Custom Keto Diet is more effective when compared to other Custom Keto Diet programs, and this has helped thousands of men and women lose weight quickly and effectively.

Also, several professional athletes, celebrities, nutritionists, and chefs have personally tried the Custom Keto Diet Plan program and came back with good results.

[Click Here to Order Custom Keto Diet Plan from the Official Website](#)

What does the Custom Keto Diet include?

When you purchase the Custom Keto Diet, you will get an 8-week customized meal plan designed specially by experts. There is a panel of fitness trainers, chefs, and nutritionists making sure that the plan is designed only after taking into account your overall health, and your choice of foods.

The plan includes foods you can eat and avoid. And no, it is not about eating less. It is about eating food properly, and avoiding carbs, and sticking to healthier alternatives in your diet. This makes your diet more enjoyable and you are likely to stick to it for longer. The meal plan is customizable as per your taste. It comes with instructions that help you keep your diet in order and make it free from any sort of confusion.

There are several recipes in the Custom Keto Diet program, and each recipe that is designed comes with detailed instructions. You can even make this food at home, with little to no chef experience. The plan also provides a list of groceries that you can easily purchase from your local stores.

You need not worry about having a limited choice in planning out meals, as there is a wide variety of plans listed in the program that you can choose from.

>>>Click Here to order Custom Keto Diet Plan From The Official Website

Features of Custom Keto Diet Plan

- One of the primary features of the program is how they provide you with an 8-week meal plan that is organized according to your physique and choices.

- You get a diet that is tailored accurately for your body's calorie intake and activity levels.
- Recipes that are easy to cook and healthy. These are delicious and simple and do not require one to be a pro at cooking.
- A set of guidelines that helps you to customize these recipes into essential meals.
- Several meals plans with a variety of foods so that you will not get bored eating the same thing.
- Every recipe comes with clear instructions that make your cooking experience enjoyable and hassle-free.
- The plan also provides you with a grocery list that makes shopping easy for you. These groceries are all easily available in your local stores.

Why should I buy the Custom Keto Diet?

The point of following a diet is so that you become fit. With the help of a plan, it becomes easier and more practical to stick to a diet. Custom Keto Diet helps someone who chooses to follow the Ketogenic diet.

If you are someone finding it hard to practice your diet, then with the help of Custom Keto Diet, you will be able to bring about consistency in your diet. You also have an idea of what nutrients you need to intake and how to chart out your meals and workout routines.

The Custom Keto Diet plan aids your weight loss process into a systematic model that ensures you do not break your diet.

Is the Custom Keto Diet optimal for everyone?

Any adult can use this diet plan if they want to adopt the ketogenic diet in their lifestyle. This diet, however, is best avoided by pregnant and nursing women who might need extra nutrition. This diet plan can be used by anyone interested in eating healthier and improving their quality of life via the ketogenic diet.

The diet isn't a bad way to start living healthy. Whether you're young or old, you can implement it in your life.

However, it is advised that if you have a medical condition existing, it is best to consult your doctor before you start the diet as it may otherwise affect your health. It is also advised that anyone below the age of 18 keep away from the diet. This plan is not designed for minors and they require a different level of nutrients.

Custom Keto Diet Benefits

- It increases the fat-burning process. A ketogenic diet helps to drop insulin levels. This helps to burn fat easily. Your body does not have sufficient carbs to produce energy and hence converts the excess fat into energy. This burns your fat and helps in weight loss.
- The keto diet is easy to follow and helps you balance your meals with food you love that is healthy. This helps you not to burden yourself with the diet. They are tailor-made for you and hence make it easy for you.
- Your appetite is limited and you won't have excessive

cravings. The diet is designed with meals that will help you feel full easily. This will cut down your appetite which eventually helps you to cut down your calorie intake which is an important advantage mentioned in this custom keto diet reviews.

- There are no hardcore gym routines that you have to follow. The diet practice is plenty enough. Your workout can be a moderate one with no back-breaking regimes.
- The diet program is healthy and safe to practice. As the diet is exclusive to what your body demands there is no side effect and harm to your body.
- You start losing weight rapidly. With the Custom Keto Diet Plan, you will notice how you are losing weight in the first few weeks itself. It is an organic process and takes time but the process will help you lose weight and not gain it back. It provides a long-lasting result.
- You can build an overall healthy lifestyle. You control your blood sugar levels, your blood pressure levels, and also your cholesterol levels with the help of a Custom Keto Diet plan.
- It comes with a 100% money-back guarantee that ensures your refund if you are unhappy with the supplements.
- You can easily find the groceries in your local stores and the recipes are easy to make while being healthy.

How do you get your hands on this?

It is available on their official page only. If you wish to customize a diet plan, you need to visit their official

<u>website</u>. You may come across several websites offering attractive discounts and guarantees but those are not legit. The official website has not authorized access for sale to any other website.

The program was originally priced at $97 but now there is a discount on their website and you can customize your keto diet plan for $37. The site also provides a 60-day money-back guarantee that offers you a 100% refund if you are unhappy with the diet plan.

Is Custom Keto Diet Plan legit?

From the studies and reviews, I would say that the plan is legit. There is nothing that looks shady about this plan and it has shown successful results for many of its users.

You may come across some websites that try to trick you into a sham by giving you a fake keto diet plan. There are non legit sites that try to steal your money and personal information. It is advised to stay away from these sites and purchase only from their official page.

Custom keto Diet Customer Reviews and Complaints

There have been no complaints as of now in regards to the program. The customer reviews also shed a positive light on the Custom Keto Diet plan and talk about how the plan has helped people find a great deal of success in maintaining their diet.

Final Thoughts on Custom Keto Diet Review

The Keto diet is pretty popular in the US due to its successful weight loss effect. The diet has been followed by many individuals as they do not have to go through drastic changes. The diet is easy to customize as well. For a fresher, it can be a little overwhelming if they do not have a proper guide. With a Custom Keto Diet plan, this is made easy.

As explained in this Custom Keto Diet review, you get to improve your diet and lose weight rapidly if you are consistent with the plan. It comes with a list of recipes, groceries, and meal plans which are charted to fit exclusively for your body.

You also are guaranteed a 100% refund if you are unhappy with the plan. If you are looking into the ketogenic diet and think a plan would help you kick start your healthy routine, I'd suggest you give Custom Keto Diet plan a try if you are convinced.

Frequently Asked Questions by our Audience

- **Is it safe to practice the program?**

The Custom Keto Diet is a healthy and safe program to practice if you are someone following the keto diet. With the help of the program, you can keep up consistency in practicing the diet which healthily aids weight loss.

- **Is there any additional charge?**

There are no additional charges like subscription fee, delivery or shipping fee, service fee, etc. You only have to pay while placing the order and the program will be mailed to you free of cost.

- **What do I do if I am not happy with the program?**

You can request a refund if you are dissatisfied with the program. It is a hassle-free process and you will receive 100% of what you invested.

- **Can I use the program even if I am above 50?**

The Custom Keto Diet is designed for adults irrespective of their age. Hence you can use the plan even if you are 50 plus. The plan will be customized concerning your age and so it will not affect your health.

[>>>Click Here To Get Custom Keto Diet Guide From The Official Website](#)

About Consumers Companion

Consumers Companion is an e-commerce news and product review website for dietary supplements including vitamins, and we are dedicated to presenting only the most effectual supplements manufactured by the most trusted brands in the industry.

We're dedicated to giving information about products that facilitate your health. Each natural supplement, you'll find on our website have been judged by our research team for its quality. Every product we highlight is backed by a money-back guarantee and our secure website confirm a safe shopping practice for our customers. In addition, our knowledgeable experts are ready to clarify all your doubts and help you gain better health.

It's sometimes hard to cut through all the junk that's out there when all you require is a solution to your trouble. Marketing professionals have knowledge about the health issues people have and they take advantage of our strong desires to gain better health.

>>>Click Here To Get Custom Keto Diet Guide From The Official Website

Custom Keto Diet is newly introduced by a fitness expert Rachel Roberts, offering a customized keto diet plan based on a person's goals, fitness, taste buds, and body type. This diet plan is not like the ordinary hundreds and thousands of recommended plans hovering in the market that do nothing as promised; Custom Keto Diet is using a whole different approach to help people attain a desired summer body. This Custom Keto Diet Review intends to reveal everything one needs to know about the plan.

The Custom Keto Diet works by targeting the weak areas and prepares body to be in a working mode. The key to using this diet plan is to be consistent. The Custom Keto Diet is not for you if you cannot be consistent and are not determined towards your goal. Stay consistent and leave the rest on the Custom Keto Diet plan.

Product Description – Custom Keto Diet by Rachel Roberts

The **Custom Keto Diet** sets its base on a keto diet, a scientifically proven method to lose weight effectively in a span of total 8 weeks.

This incredible 8-week plan can be of great use for any gender, age, or body type. Rachel Roberts' diet plan sets the body on a long-term fat loss goal.

The diet plan is set by experienced trainers, chefs, and nutritionists. You even get a downloadable grocery list to save time and make your dream figure come true. What is more? You will get instant access to the plan right after you follow the steps discussed below.

Why Choose the Custom Keto Diet?

The Custom Keto Diet does not make fake promises and aims to help you at every step. They welcome their customers to contact them at any query at any time.

After you fill the questionnaire, you will be moreover able to check the summary of what your body needs. It lists down the recommended calories, BMI, water intake, activity level, and the approximate weight you will be able to achieve after 30 days of use of the Custom Keto Diet. It even shares the amount of fat, protein, and carbs you should take every day.

You will be able to customize your diet plan according to your needs. There is now no need to worry about investing in nutritional and weight loss supplements. The 60-day plan makes things easy and serves you in its best way.

The <u>Custom Keto Diet</u> also shares the trending keto diet and portion sizes that are best for your body and health. With step-by-step instructions, the recipes in the diet plan are simple and easy to handle. What features make it further unique? To find out more, have a look below at the next heading.

Some Unique Features of the Custom Keto Diet

Some of the unique features that set the Custom Keto Diet apart from other diet plans on the market are:

1. Edit and Customize According to Your Needs

Customize Keto Diet uses sophisticated and friendly algorithms to prepare your 8-weeks plan. If you want to edit the plan on your side, the algorithm will again make a quick calculation to set your plan at its best level.

2. Fast Food Eateries

Custom Keto Diet is extremely user friendly and thinks of its utmost duty to care about the satisfaction of their customers. Therefore, they completely understand that there may be situations where you would like to eat outside. It is the only keto diet plan, which allows you to eat only the KETO-FRIENDLY FOOD from your favorite restaurants like Mcdonalds, Wendys, Burger King, Subway, In & Out Burger, and many more.

3. Intermittent Fasting

If you are not in a mood to eat anything and want to skip a meal, no issue. The Custom Keto Diet adjusts itself so that you can easily plan out your eating rather than being pressurized to eat.

Steps to Buy a Successful 8-Week Plan

To buy a Custom Keto Diet plan you need to click the link here and follow the steps below. You will have immediate access after the confirmation of your order. Start now.

Step #1

Step one asks you to fill out the basic information to get a better of your situation and needs. Try to be honest; otherwise, this product is totally a failure for you. It asks about your gender, your daily activity, preferred meat. Make sure you type the email address correctly, as you will only receive your 8- week plan over there.

Step #2

As soon as the questionnaire is filled, an immediate diet plan is offered to you. To complete the process, at last, enter your card details.

Step #3

Rise and shine. The final step is to put the plan into action. Follow your Custom Keto Diet plan and wait for the magic to occur.

What are the Options Offered in the Custom Keto Diet?

The Custom Keto Diet is an 8-week plan, which rather than being harsh on your body prefers your body flexibility. It makes sure to give you a satisfying experience by not crossing the extent of load your body can bear in 8-weeks. Even vegetarians and the allergic can use the Custom Keto Diet. Ready to make a change? Great! This is how the Custom Keto Diet works.

Option #1 – Activity Section

The daily activity section asks your intensity of daily work by giving you several options, which include being a couch potato, somewhat active, average activity, very active, and extremely active.

Option #2 – Food Section

It further questions the type of meat you would like to include in your diet plan. The options given are chicken, fish, pork, beef, no meat, and bacon.

The veggie section includes broccoli, cauliflower, avocado, zucchini, asparagus, and mushrooms. It is important to select at least one veggie to make your Custom Keto Diet work.

It also offers other healthy foods you would like to have in your diet like coconut, eggs, cheese, butter, nuts, and cottage cheese.

Is the <u>Custom Keto Diet</u> Pocket Friendly?

The Custom Keto Diet, besides being effective and unique, is affordable too. The $97 diet plan on the current discount is being sold out at $37 only. The product is backed up with 3750 customer reviews and a 4.5-star rating.

Yes! You heard it right that you do not have to pay any extra for the subscriptions. The program is a one-time payment only. Set your life and achieve optimal weight with lifetime access by the Custom Keto Diet. In case, at any time you feel unsatisfied with the product, you can shoot them an email and get all your money back.

Final Thoughts on the Custom Keto Diet

Investing in the **Custom Keto Diet** for a perfect figure is a smart choice to make at times like this when you can't go out to gym.

It is now easier than ever before to beat the transformation challenge with the Custom Keto Diet. The Custom Keto Diet is a great opportunity to put your goals into action. It gives you a grocery list, ready to make plans, clear step-by-step instructions, a wide range of foods to choose from, and whatnot.

Contents

www.ingramcontent.com/pod-product-compliance
Lightning Source LLC
Chambersburg PA
CBHW060947130726
48001CB00003B/1101